149 EPIC
BACKLINKING
STRATEGIES

YOUR SECRET LINK BUILDING
TOOLBOX FOR OFF-PAGE SEO

Get Access to the Ultimate List of
Off-Page Search Engine Optimization
Link Building Tactics

SHIVANI KARWAL

149 Epic Backlinking Strategies: Your Secret Link Building Toolbox!

First Edition

Preface

Thank you for purchasing 149 Backlinking Ideas. This book is the most complete list of link building ideas on the web!

If you enjoy reading this book, please leave a review on Amazon.

You can get in touch with me at: **shivani@digiologist.com**.

If you want to take your learning to the next level, check out my **SEO Course** at **www.digiologist.com (link to course:** https://goo.gl/C43oMO). I have a coupon code for my valuable readers for my course! Use the **coupon code *Amazon* for 75% off.**

I hope that after reading this book, you are able to experience the power of online marketing and it brings your business massive success.

Thank you for reading!

Shivani Karwal

149 Link Building Ideas

1. **Resources:** Resources pages are pages with lists of links. They're all over the web and exist for practically every industry. You can find them by inserting your keywords into search strings, a list of which you'll find in the next chapter.

2. **Unlinked Brand Mentions:** There are many times when site owners talk about your brand but they don't link back. These are called unlinked brand mentions. The fact that they mentioned your business is great but not enough to send over traffic because there is no link. Not many people reading the article will put in the effort to copy your brand name and search it to find your site. A link back is required for traffic purposes and also for backlink purposes. Getting sites with unlinked brand mentions to you to link back is an easy link building method because since those sites are already talking about you, they don't mind linking back since all the work is already done and they already know about you. You can find such mentions at a scale in just a few minutes using a few tools (tutorials are up on this and other topics in the Digiologist Marketing Course).

3. **Misspelled Mentions:** If there are more than a few ways to type your company name or even a few possible spelling mistakes, insert them

into the tools to find unlinked mentions with the wrong company name as well. This should also be done for company name variations and short forms and also previous names incase you recently changed your name.

4. **URL Mentions:** Along with finding brand name mentions, it's also important to find URL mentions i.e. when sites use your site URL into their article instead of your brand name. Though this is less common, it's still important to go after. The URLs being referred to here are the ones not resulting in hyperlinks due to a missing http:// and so, not resulting in an actual link.

5. **Track Industry Term Mentions:** Create an alert for popular industry term mentions so you know which sites are talking about specific topics in your industry. It would be a better idea to track very particular terms that are detailed so you're not bombarded with alerts. Tracking such terms will bring up prospects of sites mentioning them and possible sites and pages you can get a link from by contributing in some way.

6. **Competitors Brand Mentions:** You can't exactly get a link for your competitors brand mention, but you can track your competitors brand mentions to see where they are being linked from. Check out the sites where they're getting mentioned and try getting a link for your site from them too.

7. **Competitor Backlink Analysis:** You can use tools to get access to the entire backlink profile

4

of your competitors. After getting a list of their backlinks, sort according to quality and see which of the sites you can possibly get a link from.

8. **Competitors Common Backlink Analysis:** Involves using a tool like Majestic SEO that can look into the backlinks of a few of your competitors and find the backlinks they all have in common. Finding the sites each of your competitors has in common allows you to go after the top sites first and is faster than individual competitor analysis.

9. **Get an Indirect Backlink From Your Competitor:** It is quite common that some of your competitors link to the same sites. Link Juice Thief (LJT) finds places where your competitors commonly link to. These sites are usually big authorities in your industry. The Link Juice Thief (LJT) has a similar results matrix to the Common Backlinks Tool (CBLT). In many cases, you will find that the pages your competitors link to are authoritative sites in your niche.

10. **Competitors Newest Links:** Very often, a quick reaction can mean the difference between success and failure. On the Internet, it is pretty similar. It is extremely important to be aware of your competitor's activities. Link Alerts (LA) is a tool made to inform you about your new backlinks, but, apart from that, you can also use it to monitor your competitors. Not only will it help you find some new backlink opportunities, but it can also enable you to

discover some new sources and techniques you could use in the future.

11. **Ranking Pages Backlink Analysis:** From an SEO perspective, all sites ranking above you in the search engines for your preferred keywords are competitors. Most business think of their competitors as the ones getting more business and this is mostly in the offline sense. The competitors referred to in point #10 are the companies you feel are your competitors in whichever sense, be it in terms of more business, popularity etc. From an SEO perspective, any site that ranks above you for a preferred keyword is your competitor. Take the exact pages that rank above you and get the backlinks pointing to those pages (not the entire domain, but actual pages) and see which ones you can get a link on for yourself.

12. **Guest Posting:** Guest posting involves writing articles for other blogs in your industry with a link back to your site. This allows those other sites to get good content, and you for you to get a link to your site and incoming traffic from the site. So a win-win situation for both. Guest posting is a very common link building technique. Some say it's dead, spammy and not safe. But if done right, it can add a lot of value. What you need to keep in mind while guest posting is to post on the highest quality possible sites that are not spammy and are relevant. Relevancy is the key factor here. You don't want to guest post just for the sake of getting a link. Make value your top priority.

Guest post on sites that are relevant to your industry i.e. sites that can send relevant traffic to your site that can possibly lead to sales. The most common approach to guest posting is simply reaching out to influential blog owners in your niche. It's a great idea but getting a guest post to go live on influential blogs is not always easy. These blogs are popular and so receive hundreds of outreach emails a day requesting to guest blog for them. Some of these blogs don't even accept guest posts and clearly state that. However, to get a higher response rate, it is a better idea to reach out to sites that are actually accepting guest posts. You can find these sites quickly using search strings (which have been explained in detail later on). There are also various guest posting communities like Post Joint (postjoint.com), Guestr (guestr.com), Blogger Link Up (bloggerlinkup.com), My Blog Guest (myblogguest.com) that list out sites in need of guest posts, industry wise. Another way to find guest post opportunities is to trace your competitors guest posts and seeing which sites they've written on by checking their backlinks. You can also trace the guest post path of top bloggers in your industry.

13. **Guest Posting Communities:** Guest posting communities such as Blog Dash, My Blog Guest, Blogger Link Up etc are all sites that have lists of blogs in different niches that are accepting guest posts so the step of site prospecting is not required to be done if guest posting through these communities. Some of

these communities also allow putting a notice on them for either writers required for guest posting or sites required to guest post on.

14. **Reverse Guest Posting:** Reverse guest posting involves inviting guest bloggers to blog on your site instead of you on theirs and having them share and link to what their article on your site from their site.

15. **Private Blog Networks:** Private blog networks are a group of blogs created by the same individual for the purpose of having a group of sites to get links from to the main site. You can either create your own PBN to link to your main site or purchase a link package from a PBN owner.

16. **Get Students to Blog on University Blogs:** University and college students have access to the institutions blog portal and can be hired to do an article on your business or drop a link to your site in an already written relevant article.

17. **Sponsored Posts:** Involves sponsoring the publication of a guest post on a blog i.e. a paid guest post placement.

18. **Paid Links:** Can either be a sponsored guest post or a paid text link.

19. **Interlinking:** Interlinking is not offsite but can still add a lot of value and help in ranking. It involves linking your sites internal pages to each other. Since the links are coming from your site, you have the authority to choose their location and anchor text so take advantage of that. You can link from your highest ranking and most visited pages to

pages you want to boost, to your ranking pages to help increase their ranking further or to important landing pages. There are many choices, split test them and see what works.

20. **Broken Link Building:** There are many sites out there linking out to broken pages that are either to sites that were shut down or pages that just don't exist anymore. You can find these pages at scale for sites in your industry and inform the webmasters and request your link to be replaced in place.

21. **Competitors 404s:** Find out your competitors 404s and who links to them and ask them to link to yourself instead.

22. **Reclaim Links Pointing to 404 Pages:** If you've been making some site changes recently and deleted or moved some pages and now have a few missing pages a.k.a 404s, check to see if there are any links pointing to them and have them changed to existing and more updated pages on your site instead.

23. **Reclaim External Profile Link Pages:** People will link to you if they like your product without you even requesting a link. But at times, such naturally earned links can be pointed to your social profiles instead of your website. A lot of times people link to Twitter the most and while getting a link to your Twitter is great, it's a good idea to reclaim links to your social profiles to your website instead. At times you can even keep the link to your social profile because the webmasters just needs to add a link to your site in addition.

24. **Home Page Links to Deeper Pages:** This isn't a strategy to gain new links but is still useful. You can conduct a backlink analysis of your site and see if there are too many incoming links to the home page and contact those sites to point those already existing links to deeper and more relevant pages for a more mixed link portfolio.

25. **Nofollow to Dofollow:** This isn't a strategy to gain new links but is still useful. You can conduct a backlink analysis of your site and see if there are too many incoming no-follow links to the home page and contact those sites to change them to do-follow so link juice can pass. Don't go overboard with this because it's a good idea to have some no-follow links as well for a natural link portfolio. But if any high authority sites have provided your site with no-follow links, it doesn't hurt to ask them to change them.

26. **Forum Commenting:** Forum link building is similar to Q and A sites. Forums are like online groups. They're created for a specific industry where people post threads to ask questions, ask for opinions, or simply just discuss a particular topic. You can become a member of a few of the main forums from your industry and join in on the conversations taking place. Getting links from the forum threads is not always possible in the beginning since the admins are strict about it. But once you gain a reputation by becoming a frequent poster, you can start dropping links. Comment on popular

threads or ones you think will gain popularity soon and try linking your answer back to your business in some or the other way. Offer the thread poster help or a valuable opinion and let them know they can visit your site for more information. The thread poster and also the hundreds, if not thousands of people viewing the thread will read your answer.

27. **Forum Profiles:** Registering for forums allows each user to create a forum profile which is like a social media profile. Each forum profile has an about section and a section to add your website which should be filled.

28. **Blog Commenting:** This is something a lot of people do naturally. We all read many blog posts a day to do our share of industry reading. Why not leave a comment after reading while you're on the page? Try not to leave spammy links in every comment though. Most commenting systems such as Disqus let users profiles link to their sites, so you end up getting a link that way. You can provide a valuable point not discussed in the article or give your opinion so it stands out and gets noticed by people reading the comments. We often underestimate the number of people who read comments on an article and because of that blog commenting is often overlooked, but give it a try.

29. **Q & A Sites:** These links aren't the highest quality for backlink purposes but they can be huge for increasing incoming traffic. Q and A sites like Yahoo Answers, Quora etc. get a

large number of hits a month so build a presence there. Find questions related to your industry that have been asked and answer them. You answer the question and so help someone, end up being perceived as the expert and get a link back to your site. If you provide value to others through helpful answers, they will make their way to your site and your traffic (and hopefully leads) will increase. A sneaky little trick is to post a question yourself and answer it yourself as well. But use different accounts for that so it looks natural ofcourse. This Q and A thread may be made up but it will still be valuable to the others reading it as they're searching for answer to that question.

30. **Link Reclamation:** Some of the links you previously built or earned may go missing with time. This could be due to pages removed from the sites of previous linkers or they could go lost during their site redesign processes. You can always reach out to them and ask for a link again in some way. You don't have to manually keep a check on this. Upload all links built and earned into Raven Tools and it will automatically notify you each time a link is removed.

31. **Link Re-purposing:** This isn't a technique to build new fresh links, but rather repurpose old ones. You may have most of your link pointing to your home page or even an old landing page that might not even exist anymore. You can reach out to the site owners linking to you and

have them link to a different page instead that is a more important internal page. It's a good idea to have your links pointing to your home page as well as deeper internal pages. But if too many of them point to your home page, go for some diversity and request some of them to be changed.

32. **Anchor Text Re-purposing:** Changing 'click here', 'site' anchor texts to more descriptive ones.

33. **Get Local Library Links:** Libraries usually have a link page on their site to act as a resource for the general public as a compilation of professionals from different industries. Check out your local library's website and see if you can get listed on it.

34. **Expired Domain Link Building:** Sites become expired and shut down all the time. You can take advantage of that and either purchase those domains and redirect to your site (more info on that in point #35) or simply check their backlinks and request the sites linking to them to link to you instead. This only works and is worth doing if the expired sites are in the same industry as you. It can work with sites in adjacent industries as well. These links are also easy to get because the site owners are informed they're linking to expired domains so they're interested in removing the link immediately and mostly open to replacing it with your link in exchange for the help.

35. **Moved Sites:** Some businesses close or move to other sites, leaving their old site behind and

expired. Register any such sites from your industry that have a good backlink profile and use them to your advantage. You can either use those domains for building a site and linking to yourself from it, or simply redirecting it to a relevant page on your site.

36. **Non-existent Service Pages:** Find pages or sites that used to offer a service but no longer do and have their backlinks pointed to your site instead. Businesses get shut down or have some of their products/services removed all the time. If you find out about something shut down in your industry and the particular page or site that used to represent it has a good number of backlinks, inform the site owners they're linking to a removed product/service and have them replace the link to your existing product instead.

37. **Expired Blogspot Blogs with Good Backlinks:** Blogspot is a blogging platform providing free hosting. It uses a .blogspot domain that looks something like: www.example.blogspot.com. The great thing about blogspot is that when a user shuts their blog, their blogspot address is available for anyone to register. And it's free. You can take advantage of that by registering shut down blogpost blog addresses that had some good backlinks.

38. **Find Sites With Spammy Links:** Similar method to malware and broken links, find sites in your industry with spammy backlinks using a backlink checker and inform them about it.

39. **Find Sites With Malware:** Malware is a hostile software causing viruses and computer damage. Using tools, find sites with malware and contact the owners and let them know about it. This puts you in their good books and is more likely to get you a link. This is similar to broken link building.

40. **Get your own Wikipedia Page:** If you've built enough authority, get yourself a Wikipedia page. Just have someone else write it for you so it looks natural and is unbiased.

41. **Content Gaps:** Filling content gaps involves improving the content on topics in your industry on other sites. There's plenty of content out there that is incomplete and could just use a few additions to improve it. You being the industry expert can reach out to those sites with additional information and be quoted as a source or score yourself a link in some other way such as through a guest article or on their blogroll.

42. **Content Updating:** Involves updating old and outdated content on topics in your industry on other sites. You can reach out to those sites with the latest up to date information on the subject and be quoted as a source or score yourself a link in some other way such as through a guest article or on their blogroll.

43. **Content Improvement:** Find a piece of content that has a ton of links. Create a better version of it. Alert the sites linking to it that you've built a better piece of content.

44. **Content Curation:** Content curation involves finding the best content on the web, compiling it and sharing it with your network. There are various sites you can use for this, one of them being Scoop.it. Create an account on them and post curated content regularly to build a following. Once you've created a following, you then have access to a network of people interested in your industry that you can post your content to whenever you need to.

45. **Link Poaching:** Link poaching involves having your competitors backlinks replaced to links pointing to your site instead. It's sneaky and even a little mean. But if you can provide sites that are linking to your competitors sites with better content to link to on your site instead and replace the links, just think of it as adding more value to those sites for their readers. Be careful about this though. You may not want to have all of your competitors links replaced and start a war.

46. **Content Link Replacements:** This is similar to link poaching, except that it doesn't involve stealing your competitors links but just links to other content. Find content in your industry that ranks well and you have a substitute for on your blog, get a list of its backlinks, reach out to the sites linking to that content and let them know that you have a similar article that is a better and a more updated version that they can link to instead. You mainly just find content that is ranking, make it better and ask people

linking to it to link to your updated and better content.

47. **Content Syndication:** Involves signing up for a syndication service or manually uploading your blog content to third party sites such as web 2.0s, press release sites, article directories etc to increase the exposure and readership of it.

48. **Create Great Content and Ask for Links:** One of the simplest ways of link building is to just create linkable content. Create assets that are link worthy. This could be in the form of eBooks, whitepapers, infographics, guides, market research studies/ surveys or just blog articles. It doesn't have to be super fancy and lengthy. Just provide value and make it better than your competitors so people see why they should link to you.

49. **Dead Content Recreation:** This involves offering to update old content out there on other sites that is outdated. Find content from your industry that was written a few or many years ago, reach out to the webmasters and offer to give them an updated version. This works well not only for old content, but also content on different strategies/ techniques/technologies from your industry that are now obsolete and replaced with something more updated.

50. **Link Roundups:** These are compilations of great links on a certain topic you can put together on your blog. These can be lists of great articles that recently came up in your

industry or links to niche influencers sites. After you're done publishing your roundup, contact the people linked to in it. They will appreciate the mention and most will either link back to your roundup article or at least socially share it.

51. **Check Copyscape for Copied Content:** Everything that you put out on the web has chances of being stolen. Keep a check on which of your content gets copied and posted on other sites. If you're sensitive about it you can just ask those site owners to remove the content. But if you're more concerned with getting a link, reach out to the sites and ask for your site to be linked to and quoted as the source of that content. Ideally you don't want entire articles of yours to be posted elsewhere as Google treats it as duplicate content and it's not favored. So if possible, try to have portions of the original content used instead of the entire article.

52. **Content Available for Reuse:** Available for re-use by linking back.

53. **Add A Snippet Feature to Your Content:** Uploading your content online will attract people stealing your content no matter what. People will right click and save and republish elsewhere. A trick to try to get a link while they do that is adding snippets to your content. That way, along with picking up your content, the person also copies a link back (and also a short summary) to your site along with it.

54. **Contact People Using Your Images:** Similar to using Copyscape to check people using your

content, use image source checker tools like Tineye to find people who have used your images without permission. If you're sensitive about it, you can ask them to remove the images but if you want a link, you can have them add a link back to you under the image and quote you as the source for the image.

55. **Get Image Hotlinkers to Link to You:** Image hotlinking involves displaying images on your site that belong to another site and are displayed by linking to the image on the other site without having to save and upload the image. It is also referred to as inline linking. When the website with the hotlinked image is opened, the image is displayed but it is actually loaded from the site where it is originally located. Note that this also uses up more bandwidth from your site so if you want to prevent that, you can disable hotlinking altogether. If you're okay with giving up a bit of bandwidth in exchange for backlinks from hotlinkers, you need to enable a script. This can be done easily using a plugin.

56. **Offer Images to be Used With Credit:** In addition to providing image embed codes and getting credit from those using your images without permission, it's a good idea to simply offer your images for use as well. When you offer them, more people will know they're available for use and they are more likely to end up on sites and so, more links obtained. Just put giving credit through a link back as the

source as the criteria for being allowed to use your images.

57. **Embed Codes (Images, Content, Videos):** Similar to using snippets for content, add image embed code options under every image. This will give people the option of using the images on their site using the embed code instead of saving and uploading them. This also straight away gives them permission and encourages them to use the images. You automatically get a link back from the embed codes used and you can set that up by creating custom codes through Embedly (www. embed.ly).

58. **Reverse Image Searches:** Similar to finding sites that have copied your content, it involves finding sites that have used your images without permission using a tool like TinEye. You can either have those sites remove the images or turn it into a link building opportunity and ask those sites to link to you and give you credit by listing your site as the source of the image.

59. **Ask for Links from Partners and Vendors:** Have vendors you frequently purchase from? You've already built the relationship so leverage it and get a link out of it. You can ask to be places on their 'friends page' if they have one or offer to write them a testimonial for their site.

60. **Ask People You Know for a Link:** People you know refers to your friends. Think about all the friends you have and all the contacts you've

built through networking that have their own businesses whose sites you can get a link from.

61. **Previous Linkers:** Check your backlinks and see if any previous linkers are interested in linking to your site again.

62. **Ask Your Customers:** Ask your best customers which business they're in and see if getting a link from them is possible. Often times your customers have their own business too and can give you a link if relevant.

63. **Transcribe Videos:** Transcribing videos involves making a transcript of the content of the video i.e. producing a written version of the videos content. Find YouTube videos in your industry that have done well, contact the owner and ask them if they'd like you to transcribe the video so they can use the written version of the video on their blog. This would be useful to them because the written version of the video as a blog article would also have chances of doing well. Also, it is something that's easy for you to produce and can be done from Fiverr and relevant websites for just a few bucks. Transcribing other site owner's videos is a way to get links by helping others. It's a fast way of relationship building that gets you links back in return some or the other way.

64. **Blog Post Translation:** If your blog is in English, have some of your blog posts shared on other sites in other countries in other languages after translation. Some popular language choices other than English would be

Mandarin and Spanish, which are the most spoken languages globally before English. This can be like a guest article, except that you're not writing new content but just repurposing old content and making it new through translation. This is great for businesses that have their product/service available worldwide so they can target audiences in other countries.

65. **Translating Content:** Similar to transcribing content, translating content produces another version of the same content as well. Offer to translate other people's popular blog posts into other languages such as from English to Mandarin, Spanish etc., so they can avail benefit from those markets as well. Again, this is a strategy of link building involving helping others to build relationships that can be used to get links in return.

66. **Associations/Organizations:** Get a link from associations or organizations in your industry you're a part of or join them.

67. **Awards:** Get a link from sites of committees or organizations your business got awards from in the past.

68. **Blog Badge:** Create a blog badge and inform your readers. Your most loyal readers will share it on their sites and link back to you.

69. **Blog Carnival:** Blog carnivals are like link submission parties, except that the link needs to be to an article. Blog carnivals, which are sometimes also called blog parties, have a theme or topic announced before hand and ask for bloggers to submit articles links talking

about that topic. If you participate and submit a link to your article on that topic, you get an immediate link.

70. **Blog Incubation:** Blog incubation involves starting your own blogs to get links from. This refers to blogs separate from your main site. These are like mini blogs you make just for the sake of linking to yourself from. Keep them on topics related to your industry so the links built are relevant.

71. **Blogrolls:** Blogrolls are lists of blog owners favourite blogs. They're a way of listing out all the blogs they read and recommend to their readers. While it may be tough to get on someone's blogroll without knowing them at first, it's a good idea to build a relationship and introduce them to your blog so they see the value in adding it to their roll.

72. **Classified Ads:** You can also get links from online classified sites such as Craigslist and Kijiji. If you're from a larger, more well known company, you may not want to do this to keep up your brand image but if you're just starting out and like the sound of the idea then go for it.

73. **Job Postings:** Have an open position? Many times business owners rely on filling positions through referrals and don't post job openings online. It's a good idea to take advantage of the opening and post it on high traffic job sites like Monster, Workopolis etc. You get a link and also get more applicants.

74. **Contest/Giveaway on Other Bloggers Sites:** In addition to giving away your product/service

on your site, offer to give it as a prize for other bloggers giveaways with a rule for entry being either sharing your site socially or linking back to your site through a blog post. This way, all the participants will link back to your site in order to get an entry to the contest and so you end up getting multiple links.

Hold on...

You made it so far into this book! I'm so glad you're enjoying it!

Want to take your learning even further?

Check out my SEO Course at Digiologist.com

Course available at https://goo.gl/C43oMO

Course Details:

- 4.5 Hours of video tutorials
- 52 video lessons
- Lifetime Access
- Continually Updated

I have a special coupon code for my valuable readers only!

Use the coupon code *Amazon* for 75% off.

Course syllabus and reviews listed at the end of this book.

75. **Create Industry Tools:** Industry tools like widgets and calculators are great linkbait. They are helpful to people and so get shared and linked to easily and frequently.

76. **Display Ads:** Display ads through banners on other sites get you an immediate link. While this may be a short-term image link, it's still worth experimenting with. This can allow you get a link on some of the best blogs in your industry and for a much lower price than if you directly asked them for a link and they wanted it to be a paid transaction. This is also really good for increasing traffic and leads.

77. **Fixing Grammar/Spelling:** Grammar or spelling mistakes can be found at scale using tools so don't worry about spending hours manually looking for mistakes. Have the tool search for any errors in popular articles from your industry and if you find any errors, let the site owner know so they can correct them. They'll appreciate your help and it will be easier for you to get a link in some way from their site then from a guest post, resource page, blogroll etc. because you've helped them and built the relationship.

78. **Get Interviewed:** Offer yourself for interviews. You can reach out to industry bloggers and offer to be interviewed or find interview opportunities through PR sites. You can also follow the interview path of your competitors to see which sites they've been interviewed on and try to score an interview for yourself there

as well. All this is easier to accomplish if you've developed a bit of a following.

79. **Interview Journalists Who Cover Your Niche:** Similar to reverse guest posting, interview influential bloggers on your site instead of you being interviewed on theirs. They will appreciate it and in most cases, share a link to it on their site.

80. **Getting Trackbacks:** When you link to other bloggers from your blog articles and source them as relevant blog posts or references, you can fill their link in the trackback section. This then leaves a trackback (also called pingback) on the other bloggers article in the comments section as a link and short summary to your article. These may not always appear instantly though as some bloggers like to manually approve them. But either way, they're great for relationship building.

81. **Giving Trackbacks:** Giving trackbacks is important as well as sites like to link to sites that give out trackbacks so they can benefit from linking to you. This makes sites want to link to you.

82. **Give Product/Service for Review:** Give your product or offer your service to influential bloggers to try out and review on their end. This helps get the word out and backlinks.

83. **Give Products/Service Away in a Giveaway:** Give away your product or service in a giveaway or contest on your site. You can set sharing your site socially or writing a blog post about an industry topic with a link to your site

at the bottom as the rules for entry. This way, all the participants will link back to your site in order to get an entry to the contest and so you end up getting multiple links.

84. **Best Blogs List:** Also known as 'blogrolls', this is a list of your favourite blogs from the industry and can also be made as a list of your favorite tools, softwares etc. You can then reach out to the people listed and let them know they've been mentioned and get links in the same way as monthly/weekly 'best of' lists mentioned in the previous point would get you. Another method is to reach out to sites that have their own blogrolls and request to be listed on them.

85. **Monthly/Weekly 'Best of' List:** Create an ongoing 'best of' list either each week or month where you link to the best articles or overall blogs from your industry by compiling them into a list. This is like a round up and similar to article round ups that are one question interview style, except that with this strategy you're creating a list style compilation of your favorite links. After creating and publishing it, reach out to the people you mentioned in it and let them know you gave them a shoutout on your site. This will allow you to build a relationship with them easier and at times they will link back to the list they've been mentioned in or return the love some other way.

86. **Local Links:** It's important to search for local link opportunities while implementing different link building opportunities such as looking for

local directories and placing guest posts on local blogs etc.

87. **Offer a Scholarship:** Offer a scholarship to students from different universities having writing an essay as the criteria for entry. The students will post their essay on their blog (and create blogs incase they don't have one) and link to your site as the source of the scholarship as the rule for entry.

88. **Offer Student Discounts:** Offering student discounts is a great way to get links from university and college sites, backlinks from which are considered high in value.

89. **Phone Based Link Building:** Not exactly a link building method but this idea works extremely well. When you request for a link through a phone call rather than an email, it is a lot easier make the relationship and get the link as you can be more personable and communicate better over phone. It's not possible to pick up the phone for each link you're trying to build so do this for the top sites you're trying to get a link from.

90. **Sponsor Events:** Build relationships by sponsoring local events. The event sponsors are shown on the event site and usually linked to.

91. **Volunteering:** Volunteer to help out local charities, NGOs, organizations. This helps build relationships and it is easier getting links with those relationships. Most such organizations have a members page on their

site which they use to link to participating companies.

92. **Donations:** Through donations you build relationships and look good in the community. Philanthropy work is always appreciated. Organizations that accept donations usually have a donators list on their site where you can have yourself added and linked to after giving the donation. A good idea would be search before hand which sites offer this.

93. **PR Commenting:** Make an account on PR commenting sites like HARO (Help a Reporter Out) and Response Source. These sites have a lot of journalists sign up that are looking for opinions from specialists in different fields. You get all of the questions/topics that replies are required for from journalists and you can answer the ones related to your industry. If the journalist finds your content useful, they use it in their article and quote you and link back to your site. This is great for backlinks and excellent for traffic. At times you can get links from very reputable sites such as Huffington Post, Forbes etc. that is otherwise quite difficult.

94. **Quotes:** Find quotes from popular (but not very popular) influencers from your industry and use their quotes in articles on your site and let them know you mentioned them. Don't do this with very popular personalities though since it's difficult to contact them.

Earning links naturally by uploading link bait (high quality content worth linking to that is created to attract links) is better than link building as you don't have to ask for the links as they're organic and acquired naturally as the other person wants to link to your content. Below are some link earning methods:

95. **Blog:** Setting up a business blog on your site is bound to get you more links rather than not having one. The more content you publish, the more content other sites have to possibly link to.
96. **Infoanimations:** Infoanimations are short animated videos. They're usually a few minutes long only and are made with the same goal infographics are made with: to explain complex topics in an easier way. These again are something that not everyone is doing and have better chances of going viral.
97. **Memes:** Memes may not be suitable for all businesses but if your business isn't too formal, give memes a try instead in addition to other graphics like infographics.
98. **Infographics:** Though infographics and guest posts as strategies have been exhausted in the past, they still work, provided you do them right. Have a few infographics designed each year that are high quality and unique so they're shareable and stand out from all the other infographics out there so people want to share them. After having them designed reach out to

site owners and allow them to use the graphics on their site with a link back.

99. **Comics:** Again, not suitable for all businesses but worth a try. If done well, they have chances of going viral and they're definitely unique and not something everyone is doing.

100. **Instructional Gifs:** Instructional gifs are a very new strategy. Hardly anyone is doing them so it's a great time to jump on board. Instructional gifs are like screencast videos, except much shorter like 15- 20 seconds long. Though you can't explain in-depth and do an entire strategy tutorial, you can make these about little hacks and make multiple of them that all flow together as single steps to complete one large task.

101. **Case Studies:** A study about a topic that has been done over time with research and facts.

102. **Research Papers:** A study on a topic containing extensive research.

103. **Whitepapers:** An in-depth report created to educate the reader on the topic.

104. **Guides:** Are all in one pieces of lengthy content that explain a topic in-depth.

105. **Glossary:** A list of terms related to an industry and their definitions.

106. **Lists:** Can be a list of anything related to an industry that is useful. For example, in SEO, a list of tools would be helpful.

107. **Checklists:** A checklist can be a list of items to not forget or things to complete. For

example, in SEO a list of places on-page to place keywords would make a helpful checklist.

108. **Podcasts:** A recording or audio file on a particular topic and these are usually episodes. They're like audio presentations of articles.

109. **Webinars:** Online seminars i.e. live seminars that take place on the web and hence the name webinar.

Directory link building involves submitting your site to relevant online directories such as business directories, industry specific directories, local directories etc. Submission link building involves submitting your assets such as images, videos, slides etc to submission sites around those materials. Below are some directory and submission link building ideas:

110.   **1-800 Directories**
111.   **Alumni Directories**
112.   **App Directories**
113.   **Article Submissions**
114.   **Audio Sharing Sites**
115.   **Blog URL Directories**
116.   **Business Card Directories**
117.   **Business Directories**
118.   **Coupon Sites**
119.   **CSS Galleries**
120.   **Document Sharing**
121.   **eBook directories**
122.   **Image Submission**
123.   **Infoanimation Submissions**
124.   **Infographic submissions**

125. **Logo Gallery Directories**
126. **PDF Submisisons**
127. **Podcast Directories**
128. **Profile Directories**
129. **RSS irectories**
130. **Slide Submissions**
131. **Tool, Plugin and Widget Directories**
132. **Video Submissions**
133. **Webinar Directories**
134. **Reciprocal Link Building:** Make a deal and link to relevant sites to have them link back to you. This basically involves trading links. Do this sparingly and with caution though.
135. **Three Way Links:** A linking system that takes place between 3 sites where site A links to site B, site B links to site C and site C links to site A.
136. **Link Wheels:** A group of sites that link to each other in a strategic manner. For example, in the case of 6 sites, namely. A, B, C, D, E and F. With A being the main site, then B links to C, C links to D, D links to E, E links to F, F links to B and B links to A, thereby completing the wheel.
137. **Tiered Link Building (Link Pyramid):** A tiered link building approach where a set of tier 1 or 'base links' point to the main site, a set of tier 2 or middle links point to the tier 1 links and a set of tier 3 links which are usually low in quality but high in number, point to the tier 2 links.
138. **Testimonials:** Reach out to the sites of products/ services you regularly use for your

business and offer to provide a testimonial for their site. They'll not only use it and give you a link back from it to your site, but also appreciate it and easily accept it.

139. **Web 2.0:** This involves creating a presence on web 2.0 sites like Tumblr, Blogger, Wordpress etc. Web 2.0 sites are like free blogging platforms. You can put relevant content on them by outsourcing articles or through article spinning. Use a good quality paid article spinning tool so it results in articles that are completely different from the ones you input into it and it gives you fresh readable content. Don't go for article scraping though. Once you've built up authority and a readership on your web 2.0 properties, you can start adding links to them pointing to your main site. These links will be relevant and all in your control so you get to choose their location, anchor text etc and since the articles are spun content, you do all this through minimal effort.

140. **Adjacent Markets:** Although there are numerous link building strategies and opportunities, there will come a time when you'll exhaust your opportunities. When you do, it's good idea to look into opportunties related to adjacent markets i.e. industries that function alongside your industry as a cross dependance on one another but not in competition. For example, pens and papers. They're both different products and production industries, not competitors but are required by one another.

141.   **Press Releases:** A statement or article containing news, updates and information that is supplied to online news portals. Anytime you make any site changes, updates, release new products, you should create and send off a press release and insert a link to your site.

142.   **Alumni Profiles:** If you went to college or university, it's a good idea to join the alumni team and be given the opportunity to create a profile on the site of the institution, resulting in a .edu link.

I haven't suggested individual sites in this link building ideas list but the below 3 sites are important ones:

143.   **Gov Chamber of Commerce:** Every country's government has a website which usually lists businesses in that country and are a high authority site to get a link from by creating a profile.

144.   **Dmoz:** The oldest and most authoritative directory online.

145.   **BBB:** Stands for Better Business Bureau and is the top business directory.

146.   **Citations:** An online reference and display of your company name, address and phone number (NAP) in that particular order. Similar to link building, citations should be placed across various external sites for improving local rankings. While building citations (which are usually placed on

directories) it is easy and advised to get a link by placing the link on the same page as well.

147. **Discount Promotions:** Run a discount promotion and get listed in deal websites (i.e. redflagdeals.com in Canada).

148. **Social Bookmarking:** Webpages bookmarked on social bookmarking sites, which search engines see as quality content and a backlink.

149. **Mini Sites:** A site with a keyword rich domain linking to the main site and created to rank in search engines along with the mini site in order to capture multiple top spots in the SERPs.

Further Your Learning

If you'd like to take your learning further, I have an SEO Course up on my site and more books:

Other products:

SEO Course:

Digital Marketing Handbook:

SEO Course Syllabus:

My SEO Course is available at **Digiologist.com** (**course page link:** https://goo.gl/C43oMO) and I have a special coupon code only for my valuable readers!

Use the coupon code Amazon for 75% off.

Course Details:

- 4.5 Hours of video tutorials
- 52 video lessons

Course Syllabus:

Setting Everything Up:

Introduction to the Course ⏱ 01:21

Methods of Digital Marketing ⏱ 03:31

How to Choose a Domain Name ⏱ 03:30

Parts of a Website Address ⏱ 05:23

How to Choose a TLD: Top Level Domain ⏱ 03:10

Different CMS Options for Your Site: Content Management Systems ⏱ 05:39

SEO Friendly Website Design and Layout Tips ⏱ 05:10

Useful WordPress Plugins for Your Site ⏱ 03:28

SEO Basics:

Introduction to SEO ⏱ 01:21

Ranking Factors Google Considers While Crawling Your Site ⏱ 07:18

Site Metrics: DA, PA, PR ⏱ 05:30

How to Check Site Metrics ⏱ 05:21

How to Create Search Strings for Targeted Searches ⏱ 09:52

How to Create Multiple Search Modifiers for Advanced Searches ⏱ 05:58

On-Page SEO:

Introduction to On-Page SEO ⏱ 01:06

SEO Friendly Site Structure: Do's and Don'ts ⏱ 05:41

How to Create a Sitemap ⏱ 04:32

How to Create a Robots.txt File ⏱ 04:39

Finding Site Errors and How to Use Redirects: 301s, 302s, 404s ⏱ 04:09

Keyword Research: Introduction ⏱ 05:28

Keyword Research: In-Depth Demonstration ⏱ 18:05

Optimizing On-Page SEO Elements ⏱ 07:38

Off-Page SEO: Link Building

Introduction to Off-Page SEO ⏱ 00:59

100+ Link Building Strategy Ideas: Part 1 (Idea #1 to Idea #30) ⏱ 16:31

100+ Link Building Strategy Ideas: Part 2 (Idea #31 to Idea #60) ⏲ 15:52

100+ Link Building Strategy Ideas: Part 3 (Idea #61 to Idea #128) ⏲ 08:43

Link Earning Ideas ⏲ 07:15

Anchor Text Usage While Building Links ⏲ 06:40

Nofollow Links vs Dofollow Links ⏲ 03:01

What a Good Link Looks Like ⏲ 00:54

Creating and Using Search Strings to Find Link Opportunities ⏲ 06:47

Guest Posting Tutorial ⏲ 19:59

Unlinked Brand Mentions Tutorial ⏲ 06:48

Resource Link Building Tutorial ⏲ 10:27

Competitor Backlink Analysis Tutorial ⏲ 03:23

Internal Linking Tutorial ⏲ 04:11

Roundup Posts Tutorial ⏲ 03:56

Using Expired Domains & Shut Down Businesses for Link Building ⏲ 03:29

Reclaiming Links to Social Profiles and 404s ⏲ 03:34

Conduct Reverse Image Searches: Find Sites Using Your Images Without Permission ⏲ 02:26

PR Commenting for Getting Media Mentions 📝 (Written Lesson)

Q and A Sites and Forum Link Building ✎ (Written Lesson)

Directory and Submission Site Link Building ✎ (Written Lesson)

Conducting Automated Customized Bulk Outreach for Link Requests ⏱ 03:14

Recording Links Built Properly and Getting Notified of Links Deleted/Removed ⏱ 01:01

Local SEO:

Introduction to Local SEO ⏱ 01:59

Setting up Your Google My Business Page ⏱ 00:50

Location Targeted On-Site Optimization and Getting Local Links ✎ (Written Lesson)

Formatting Your NAP for Citation Building ⏱ 03:12

Finding Sites to Build Citations On ⏱ 02:32

Getting Google Plus Reviews ✎ (Written Lesson)

Wrap Up ✎ (Written Lesson)

Course available at https://goo.gl/C43oMO

Use the coupon code *Amazon* for 75% off.

Course Feedback:

Great course for beginners to intermediates SEO's. I've completed lots of course's over there year but this course teaches SEO in a unique way and managed to demonstrate areas in SEO that other courses are scared to touch. ~ Omid Irani

I loved this course because the instructor make everything easy to follow. The lessons were well made and I would recommend this course to anyone who wants to understand SEO. Just do it! ~ Juanita Abenaa

Great course. I learned a lot about on-page, off-page, keyword research. This course covers all SEO. Totally worth my time and investment. ~ Ezekiel Sokoh

I Learned a lot of fresh ideas in these videos. Very useful. You are an amazing instructor with great insights! ~ Moin Sheikh

The instructor Shivani is very well spoken, very clear and very concise. She goes in to great detail explaining all the details. The videos are great in both content and quality, and the format of the learning slides is a very sleek clean design. I would highly recommend this course to anybody

wanting to learn some SEO. Thanks Shivani. Keep up the good work. ~ David Gunner

Very informative course! One of the best SEO courses I've seen here. I love how it takes you from the extreme basics to more intermediate material very smoothly so anyone can take this course up. Highly recommend to anyone looking to build up their SEO skills beyond just the basics. ~ Rick Sharma

This course is clear with professional explanations from "Shivani Karwal". I didn't understand SEO before but this course has really helped! ~ Salem Ameziane

Focused, organized, content rich and moves at excellent pace ! Very engaging! ~ Robert Smith

Informative and useful. Excellent delivery. Thank you! ~ Soon Kheng

Fantastic quality course. It may be small but it is very powerful. Thank you Shivani. I highly recommend this course to anybody wanting to advance in SEO. ~ Gonzague Re

Course available at Digiologist.com (course page link: https://goo.gl/C43oMO)

Use the coupon code *Amazon* for 75% off.

44

Other Books by Shivani Karwal:

Digital Marketing Handbook:

Available at https://goo.gl/ntyCNh

SEO Dictionary:

Available at https://goo.gl/ZnerYZ

See the table of contents and reviews for the Digital Marketing Handbook in the next few pages.

'Digital Marketing Handbook' Table of Contents:

'Digital Marketing Handbook' available for purchase on Amazon at https://goo.gl/ntyCNh

Digital Marketing Handbook Book Feedback:

This book is an incredible wealth of knowledge! Some of the information was a complete eye opener for me. This book is loaded with information and is divided nicely into 5 books covering various aspects of digital marketing with nice lists of industry tools, FAQ sections, how-to tutorials. This book was really informative and I'll be using a lot of the learnings from it for my site. ~ Amazon Customer

Simple and easy to understand. ~ Amazon Customer

Quite informative. Starts off really basic but then gets into some very useful stuff. ~ Steve Williams

Most marketing books are full of fluff, but this book is one of the most practical that I have read since I began my studies in Marketing. As a young professional, I haven't yet gotten the chance to accumulate much professional experience in digital marketing. However, this book has it all. Tips, suggestions, software and plugin recommendations- every little technical point you need to get your feet off the ground and become an effective digital marketer. It has all the rules and best practices to follow for SEO, PPC, etc. Easily translatable into the professional workplace, you'll feel super confident about digital marketing strategy after reading it. 5 star rating-was definitely worth my time and money. ~ Sarah Mancini

Great read! It was very insightful and had everything I needed to start my career in digital marketing. I highly recommend this handbook to anyone looking to increase their company's online presence or looking to enter this exciting field. ~ Amazon Customer

We've purchased approximately 10 books on this subject. This is by far the best in class. Simple, but effective! ~ Dino Trakakis

This book is awesome! Its super easy to understand and makes digital marketing so simple. It was the best choice I could have made. I'm new to the SEO world and I was looking for something that could help me to understand the basics. I love this book and it has given me

awesome foundation for my digital marketing career! ~ Juanita Abenaa

Available for purchase on _Amazon_ at https://goo.gl/ntyCNh

Final Thoughts

I hope you now have a better idea of SEO and some strategies you can implement for your business. I hope this book helps you in building a stronger digital profile for your business.

If you enjoyed reading this book please consider reviewing it on Amazon.

In case of any questions or feedback, you can email me at shivani@digiologist.com.

Thanks for reading!

- Shivani Karwal